A Bilingual Book
English/Español

Baby Moses

Bebé Moisés

i can read **Bible Stories**

Rose Tooley Gamblin

Autumn House® Publishing
www.autumnhousepublishing.com
A Division of **REVIEW AND HERALD® PUBLI...**
Since 1861

Published by Autumn House® Publishing, a division of Review and Herald®
Publishing, Hagerstown, MD 21741-1119

Autumn House® titles may be purchased in bulk for educational, business, fund-
raising, or sales promotional use. For information, please e-mail
SpecialMarkets@reviewandherald.com.

Autumn House® Publishing publishes biblically based materials for spiritual,
physical, and mental growth and Christian discipleship.

The author assumes full responsibility for the accuracy of all facts and quota-
tions as cited in this book.

This book was
    Edited by Jeannette R. Johnson
    Translated by Loron Wade
    Designed by Patricia Wegh and Heather Rogers
    Art by William Dolwick
    Typeset: Clearface Regular 16/24 (Spanish) NB Helvetica Narrow Bold
12/14

PRINTED IN U.S.A.

11 10 09 08 07   5 4 3 2 1

Library of Congress Cataloging-in-Publication Data

Gamblin, Rose Tooley, 1956-   .
  Baby Moses / Rose Tooley Gamblin.
     p. cm. – (Bible stories books)
  ISBN 978-0-8127-0466-2
  1. Moses (biblical leader)—Birth—Juvenile literature. I. Title. II. Series.

BS580.M6G33 2007
2'.1209505—dc22

                         2007010346

This book is dedicated to
those who love Jesus

I have read this book all by myself!
¡He leído todo este libro!

_____

My Name / Mi nombre

_____

Date / Fecha

What I Think About This Story
Qué pienso de esta historia

_____

_____

_____

_____

Other *Bible Stories* Books:

Joash the Boy King
Esther the Brave Queen

To order, call
1-800-765-6955.

Visit us at
www.AutumnHousePublishing.com
for information on other Autumn House® products.

Dear Caring Adult:

This series of *I Can Read* books is designed to be read by the child (with a little help from you). This makes it an ideal book for those early-grade book reports and supplemental reading assignments.

What better way to soften the nighttime jitters than to tuck your child in bed with a story of hope and blessing from the Bible.

See the baby?
¿Ves al bebé?

Sister can see the baby.
La hermana puede ver al bebé.

Brother can see the baby.
El hermano puede ver al bebé.

Mother can see the baby.
La mamá puede ver al bebé.

Father can see the baby.
El papá puede ver al bebé.

The baby is Moses.
El bebé es Moisés.

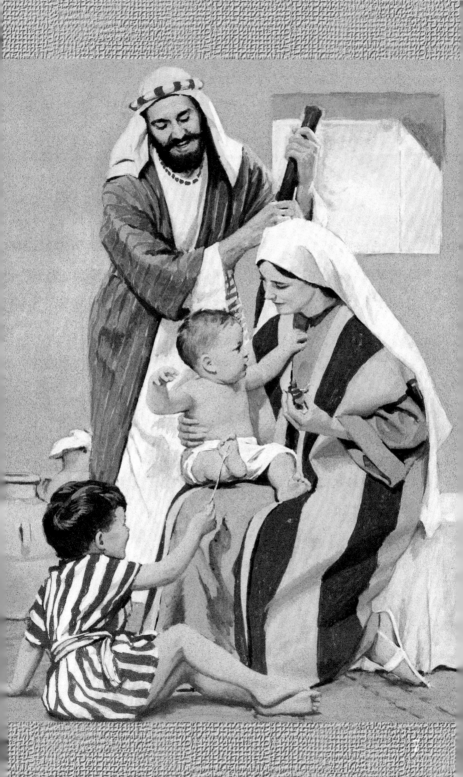

"Oh, no!" said Mother.
"¡Oh, no!", dijo la mamá.

"Oh, no!" said Father.
"¡Oh, no!", dijo el papá.

"Oh, no!" said Sister.
"¡Oh, no!", dijo la hermana.

"Oh, no!" said Brother.
"¡Oh, no!", dijo el hermano.

Who is coming?
¿Quién viene?

See the men?
¿Ves a los hombres?

See the men come.
Los hombres vienen.

The men come for
the baby.
Los hombres vienen
por el bebé.

"Sh! Sh! Baby Moses."
"¡Silencio! ¡Silencio!, bebé Moisés."

Mother can make a little boat.

La mamá puede hacer un botecito.

Sister can make a little boat.

La hermana puede hacer un botecito.

Brother can make a little boat.

El hermano puede hacer un botecito.

Make a little boat for Baby Moses.

Haz un botecito para el bebé Moisés.

Here is Sister.
Aquí está la hermana.

Here is Mother.
Aquí está la mamá.

Here is the boat.
Aquí está el botecito.

Here is the water.
Aquí está el agua.

See the water.
Mira el agua.

See the boat.
Mira el botecito.

Sister, see the little boat in the water?
Hermana, ¿ves el botecito en el agua?

Look, Sister!
¡Mira, hermana!

Who is coming?
¿Quién viene?

Oh! Oh! Oh!
¡Oh! ¡Oh! ¡Oh!

Will she see the little boat?
¿Verá ella el botecito?

Look! Look! See the little boat.
¡Mira! ¡Mira! Ve el botecito.

See the baby in the boat.
Ve al niño en el botecito.

I can see the baby in the boat.
Puedo ver al niño en el botecito.

Run, run! See Sister run!
¡Corre! ¡Corre! ¡Mira cómo corre la hermana!

See Baby Moses.
Mira al bebé Moisés.

The lady can see Baby Moses.
La dama puede ver al bebé Moisés.

Can Sister help?
¿Puede ayudar la hermana?

Here is Mother.
Aquí está la mamá.

Mother can help.
La mamá puede ayudar.

Mother can keep the baby.
La mamá puede cuidar al bebé.

See Mother and Baby.
Mira a la mamá y al bebé.

See Sister.
Mira a la hermana.

See Father and Brother.
Mira al papá y al hermano.

See Father pray.
Mira al papá orar.

See Mother pray.
Mira a la mamá orar.

See Sister pray.
Mira a la hermana orar.

See Brother pray.
Mira al hermano orar.

"Thank You, God, for Baby Moses."
"Gracias, Dios, por el bebé Moisés".

Words in This Book

a

baby (bebé)

little boat (botecito)

Brother (hermano)

can (puede)

come (venir)

coming (viniendo)

Father (Papá)

for (para)

God (Dios)

help (ayudar)

here (aquí)

I (yo)

in (en)

is (estar)

keep (cuidar)

lady (dama)

little (pequeño/a)

look (mirar)

make (hacer)

men (hombres)

Moses (Moisés)

no (no)

oh (oh)

pray (orar)

run (correr)

said (decir)

see (ver)

she (ella)

Sister (hermana)

thank (gracias)

water (agua)

who (quién)

you (tú)

Note: There are 35 words in this book. RL:1.1
Nota: Hay 35 palabras en este libro. RL:1.1

What Do You Think? / ¿Qué Usted Piensa?

1. Why do you think the soldiers wanted to hurt Baby Moses?
1. ¿Por qué usted piensa que los soldados deseaban lastimar al bebé Moisés?
2. What would you have done if you had been the sister or brother of Baby Moses?
2. ¿Qué usted habría hecho si usted hubiera sido la hermana o el hermano del bebé Moisés?
3. Why did Mother make the basket boat?
3. ¿Por qué la madre hizo un botecito con la cesta?
4. What did the lady at the water think when she saw the basket boat?
4. ¿Qué pensó la señora en el agua cuando vio el botecito?
5. How did God help Baby Moses?
5. ¿Cómo Dios ayudó al bebé Moisés?

Additional Activities / Actividades Adicionales

1. Using clay, make your favorite scene.
1. Con la arcilla, haga su escena preferida.
2. Find the country of Egypt in an atlas.
2. Encuentre el país de Egipto en un atlas.
3. Do a math project. See how many of each of the following items you can find in the book: brooms, pots, bags of grain, soldiers, pyramids, palm trees, and feather fans.
3. Haga un proyecto de matemáticas. Vea cuántos de cada uno de los puntos siguientes usted puede encontrar en el libro: escobas, frijoles, bolsas de grano, soldados, pirámides, árboles de palma, y ventiladores de pluma.
4. Find the story of Baby Moses in the Bible.
4. Encuentre la historia del bebé Moisés en la biblia.
5. Choose words from the word list and make up your won picture story.
5. Elija palabras de la lista de la palabras y haga su historia ganadora del cuadro.
6. Write a lullaby and sing it to a baby.
6. Escriba un arrullo y cántelo a un bebé.